WHATEVER

Zellia E. Fossett

Perception   Clairvoyance   Delivery

Cover Design:
Title Design/Original Artwork by Kyle Baber
kylebaber@yahoo.com
Cover Design/Original Artwork by Gwendolyn Apacanis
gapacanis@gmail.com
Graphic Design Artist/Book Cover Design by Justin Perkins
jperkinsart.com

Published by G Publishing, LLC

Library of Congress Control Number: 2018946034

ISBN: 978-0-9998578-2-3

Printed in the United States of America

I Will (love you)

I will love you.

Even as you stand imperfect.

And not only because I, myself am also imperfect

but because I want to love you.

For me

it is that simple.

For you. You know who you are.

Index

You or Whatever

Whatever is Whatever

Me or Whatever

Whatever

Me and her together.

It ain't just "whatever".

See, we have been

literally making love

between us.

a love of our own.

and we never ask

you straight people

when you first knew you were straight.

we never say

it's nasty

for you two

to make love

between you.

we never say that

your entire lives

are condemned, from above.

And that's because

we really don't care who you love.

just as long as you're a loving person.

And because

we are mad busy

being in our own love

and living.

not trying to govern another's life

or even share opinions.

We ain't just whatever.

We are not rumor.

      phase.

      or fad.

And I was raised by both

      my mom and

      dad and

they're both straight.

so, how'd I end up so

NOT?

how is it that I am

so non-straight?

It's crazy to me

that all the

"straight people"

were born "fine"

and everyone

who exists elsewhere on the

sexuality line (or spectrum)

was born

fine

and then

"something went wrong"

or

"something just ain't right or whatever."

Crazy 'cause

We ain't just whatever.

We are everything.

and you're just

"so confused",

right?

just can't wrap

your mind around

us.

as if we were

your business

to be figuring out

anyway.

my best advice

is that you

look away.

Or we can have

a stare-off

if you want.

It ain't just whatever.

This is me.

and my love.

This is us.

and my life.

These are my friends.

This is how we love.

Our whatever

is not some infatuation

for you to try to challenge.

not some freaky porno scene.

not some
onenightonavacationislandhoneydippedmidnightdream.

we are not

double-the-legs

to get between.

we are Queens.

the Only Ones capable

of birthing kings

and y'all need to show some respect.

you don't know

what I do

in bed or elsewhere.

We ain't just

whatever!

We are everything

and everything else is whatever I say it is.

God Bless 1988...

mama could not

put down the

pickle relish.

grape faygo,

other times.

papa was

forced out into

the cold

for slurpee runs.

he could not return

emptyhanded,

lest there be tears.

home-made fries

got seasoned and tossed

in barbecue sauce.

she had cravings.

mama did.

ones

that would not

let her sleep

in peace…

some mornings,

some afternoons,

most nights

her body and mind

refused to rest

without first being

satisfied.

papa might have

thought her looney,

her demands

and appetite and such.

but really,

that was me.

in there…

giving orders and throwing fits

in the dead of Winter.

mama just named me after her.

Black History

is

every

move

I make.

What I Am

If I were born any earlier in time,

I might not be any of

What I Am.

At least not outwardly.

Not in public.

Here I Am...

top of the morning

- at work
- surrounded by mostly older, white men
- reading a book

then had the nerve to wanna write

some s***

down afterward?!

- laughing to myself.

hell,

- moving... breathing...
- *being* on my own.

I wouldn't be

Any of What I Am

and so, I thank my ancestors

and wish them a good morning and a prosperous day ahead.

like I thank the older brown faces that teach me and look out
for me now.

Poetry Is...

Poetry is me talking to Jah. Me... healing.

Poetry is me being sweet. On my **Love Jones S***** "remembering love".

It's what's in me that I somehow manage to let out every now and again. Poetry is.

When I feel like the air is warm enough to sit in, with tea, I write poetry. And smile and laugh, all to myself.

Poetry is what I do when I feel like telling a story or taking a picture or painting one.

Poetry is the previews that are too good to forget. Sometimes it's the soundtrack or the credits though.

Poetry is for playing with words. Playing with my education.

Poetry is me lining up questions like dominoes. Knocking them all over, the last line of the poem being the single answer.

Poetry is for hiding secrets and disguising disappointments.

Poetry is my allergic reaction to bs.

Poetry is what I do when I need to be rude. Mummifying the depth in ambiguity. Details too. Though, in my mind, the message is loud and clear.

It's what's in me that I somehow manage to let out every now and again. Poetry is.

Poetry is what I do when I'm restless. When I'm sad about living in this world or feeling for someone else. When the bed just doesn't feel right under my weight.

Poetry is me feeling guilty, trying to act low-key.

Poetry is what I do to stop thinking. The poem is a marathon. I celebrate after, sometimes I'm exhausted but feeling accomplished.

Poetry is my heart breaking. Me gathering it up in piles. in files.

Poetry is me letting go. Getting over things. or trying to.

Poetry is everything that I am. And if I ever stop writing, don't ask me what poetry is.

I won't know.

Act On Racism

it's as if

I am a burst of light

when

black people see me.

they light up too!

giving me a greeting or hug or compliment.

it's as if

I'm invisible

when

white people—

@theeendoftheealphabet

the best

always stood last

when they all

lined up by first name,

in first grade.

the teacher always

met eyes with

the best

before a breath in

to give the class

a bundle of directions.

and it's still

that way

now.

Zellia,

comfortable and quiet,

in the teacher's

direct eye view.

Zellia,

out of her peers' reach

because

most

people tend to

overlook the kid at the end of the line.

Spelling Bee

like that time

I thought

being in a spelling bee

would be

dreadful

and I got out

on the word

"horrific".

the irony that placing third

wasn't all that bad.

The Recipe for Loving Zee

measuring cups

are irrelevant.

and all those

tools and spoons

won't help you

dig.

the words can only

bring us so close—

turn yourself (packaging) inside out for

me.

let me see.

use your intuition.

your imaginative palette.

use your whole self.

then we'll focus on portion control,

as we perfect flavor and depth.

call number

Sweet Darling…

"Hands along the spine" …

Between these towers of shelves

the research walks on stilts.

stilts.

H o l d   o n   t i g h t.

for here,

geography never sleeps

and imagination runs with wild abandon.

between these chapters

are train tracks

m   ssing tracks.

between these font-full fantasies

are brooms

sweeping over the dust of reality.

unexpected thrills

from city lights to foreign fields

lust luck love

you can feel…

with your hands along the spine.

the tall tale

may shrink

into a practical pact.

the road

may never end

and only lead to others.

the monster may retreat

just before bedtime.

riding on the margins

of each page

is choosing destiny.

hold tight.

for fiction is an amusement park

with a fancy name.

and history repeats itself—

only when we tell it to...

and the love story may meet

its parting prayer.

or the castle's cake

may fall while baking.

and crumble when icinged.

truth and lies alike

are just

call numbers.

So

hands

along

the

spine.

Let go

of this hold

when you're ready.

Remember there are fees

for damage

or disappearance.

manage your emotions

while you read.

there's the sound

of the book

hitting the bottom of the return bin.

in your ears.

be gentle.

there's the image of the bookmark.

on to the next book.

in your mind.

be kind.

We're all just call numbers

So...

hold the story right the first time around.

Your

Hands along the spine.

Choco Taco (a period poem)

Manufactured or not.

There is goodness left,

in this world we know.

can trick your brain

into believing

all is well,

when you eat chocolate.

Skate Night

the first time

I caught

The Detroit Bounce,

I woke up

the morning after

with a smile

bigger than the one

I'd ended

the night with.

Release

Reaching for the stars is more like clocking in nowadays.
Tryina find ways to beat the struggle. Income and in comes the
problems that can't be solved overnight or even explained
quite right—to the beginners. For me, this is not the starting
line. I've been reaching, higher and higher, even when I'm
sleepin' and it'll deepen once the time comes again to clock in.
My grin stays out on weekends. Widens when I give it space to
breathe. Deepens when I tell it not to leave. Happiness is this
chase, made for a daily basis. Traces of passion are keeping the
lights on. Phrases of compassion are keeping the tears at bay.
Need a 2-step or a way around this. I'm trying. Reaching while
crying. And maybe if it wasn't so systematic, I wouldn't have to
bother with the static of wanting to figure things out Now. The
stars exist to reveal natural pathways for ascendance. So, I can
fill them with all that I am afraid to release here on earth and
wait while the planet spins.

Blueberry Pie

If my soul were pie,

there'd be no

cutting you a slice.

The whole pie

is yours to take.

But I'll cut you a slice...

if you can't wait

to get me home

to have me to yourself.

Lick bits of me

off of your hands

and wrists.

I end up...

left over...

in the most

odd places on you...

find me later and

smile.

Smile, knowing the taste of my soul.

As Is

Ayo! Self!

No more negative self-talk!

I get tired of all that!

Just love me.

At least for one full day

with no complaints.

"I'm too this

and I'm too that."

"I'm not enough of this

or enough of that."

Well what am I?

What about

what I *am*

good at

and what I do

that *is* impressive?

"Where's the praise?"

You cannot claim

love

or any jones

for another

if you don't love here first.

Start with me.

As Is.

Accept me.

As Is.

Stop flashing back to

older versions

!

Love me,

if you're going to…

As Is.

After all,

I'm you

and I'm all you've got. ♡

Suave in Bed

You notice how well

your stubbornness

works for you,

early one morning,

in bed alone.

or has it worked?

you laugh in

disbelief of the

mess you've made.

your misfortunes are

dangling from the

dreamcatcher and your dreams

are catching fire,

escaping you in embers only.

good job.

real suave.

Secrets from you

I was with you after having written about you and it sort of sat with me in this weird way. Like I was keeping a secret or something. And I was. Keeping the truth about how I truly felt about you, from you... thinking "it's just easier for now".

My Best Self (to the reader)

I've given away all my real good love poems. Only the hearts they were given to will ever know how great my songs of love can grow to be. and so, when I publish about love, it seems I'm mostly disappointed in humans, though I have been loved deeply, created and made love deeply as well. I publish what is left. what matters though, is that all I ever have to say about all of it is true. you get the angle that no one else gets; ... both grateful and surprised by myself... me with my heart feeling full and with my heart feeling less than whole. you get the best of me because poetry is where I rest the best of my everything. all the things.

Orange Cranberry Tea Bags

the train ride

to Chicago

changed me.

more than because it was my first.

my mind and eyes

lost their virginity

over open, golden plains

and passing by

crumbling bridges of color

and

gaps in fields

that once were something...

made me feel silly,

thinking I'd born witness to

beauty

before that ride.

the eyes of Illinois

looked back at me.

never felt

close to the clouds

but did feel

surrounded by water.

the car coasted

like I thought

a caboose would.

reaching back into

my rolodex of yesterdays

as I sip a cup of tea.

the car coasted

because I was

present for every second.

I maybe only blinked twice.

all those hours.

I had a mason jar

filled with tea

that I never opened to drink.

my favorite kind of tea bag, floating still,

there in the jar.

I Love Your Woman

Your woman is my doctor and I love her.

Your woman is my hairdresser and I love her.

Your woman is my best coworker-friend and I love her.

Your woman is my—

... I mean,

do I

really need to

continue?...

....and there's nothing you can do to stop me.

I love your woman.

Say something.

Want You to Be My 808

You gotta know that I love you

You gotta know

And if you don't, I'll show you

Show you so

"If it's real then cling to it,

If it's artificial, let it be"

Want You To Be My 808

And complete my heart's beat

I'll hold you close when night falls

Even closer, under the sun

Wanting, every moment, for us to feel like one

I'll listen to you intently

Answer when you call

Be the one that knows how to master it all

I'll open up, just the same

To you and only you

You must believe that my heart

beats, baby, just for you

You gotta know that I love you

You gotta know

And if you don't, I'll show you

Show you so

"If it's real then cling to it,

If it's artificial, let it be"

Want You To Be My 808

And complete my heart's beat

I'm not perfect most days

And I really try to be

Wanting, every moment, to provide pleasure, to please

I'm not the most selfless

Though I do have thoughtful ways

Be the one to press the upgrade button on your day

"If it's real then cling to it,

If it's artificial, let it be"

Want You To Be My 808

And complete my heart's beat

poem inspired by The Roots' "You got me", released in 1999

Sitting Next to Strangers

Welcome to today.

Sitting alongside a stranger.

The space between us

is hello.

Very far

away from

one another.

And my wanting to write

as opposed to being glued

to the screen

of my mobile device...

probably makes people

think whatever

but the truth—

which is that I just

feel like writing...

I don't have any inkling

to consider writing about them.

but they keep looking at me.

I Had to Come Out

I used to hold

my love for women

like a secret.

It was in my

back pocket,

as far as I was concerned.

Then it started to

show in my eyes.

And in my smile,

when I'd look

at the right woman.

Pride is real.

It will

make you refill

your cup of hesitation

and stand back

and watch you suffer.

The only thing stronger than it

… is love.

You're lucky enough

Consider yourself

Lucky enough

if I write about you.

Means you somehow

seeped into me

and I either

want you to stay

or want you to go

and either way I want,

I'll write it out

and let the pen decide.

Hey Miss Light Skin

She is

She wears

She has this light skin.

high yellow.

and her skin says more than hello.

and under sun,

it drinks heavily.

so heavenly...

the skin she's in.

Pieces of Paper

my denim

knows more secrets

about me

than my best, most trusted companion.

seems like I have a pocket-full of words

that I unfold

onto the nightstand as I undress.

every evening.

professing leftover love.

stretching out q u e s t i o n marks.

writing for reasons,

countless.

on a napkin

or the back of a dollar store receipt.

half a sheet or

just a piece of paper

will suffice.

memo pad.

label.

mail.

bill paper.

flyer.

anything I can get my hands on,

when I have words

to say.

this is me

seizing the day.

Zee on a Greater Love (Here's Permission Volume 2)

I broke down. I lost parts of myself. Thinking I would never love again. I'd be better if I knew more love would eventually come. Too late and damage done and here I am, remembering how I calculated wrong, recalculating love... being deserving of real love.

Yea, I think.

It's like the hopelessness made me a different me and I was mad at myself like "how dumb of you to think that was the end" but I can't get back to the old me, before the weight of the heartbreak changed me. I know now that there is love... before love... and most definitely after love.

MERCY

Making

Everything

Right

Concerning

You

Thee Art of Predilection

I'd much rather play these games.

dancing around the

possibility of a thing

is just so fun.

the concept of waging multiple, simultaneous loves...

is much more enticing

than the bland acceptance

of the reality of a

monogamy.

"the prison of love".

with its predictability...

obligatory incessancy...

its shadow over our carnal desires and

random bouts of spontaneity.

its chameleon of a blanket of security.

monogamy *is the reason why* people cheat.

it is

"the death of the true self".

the reoccurrence of sacrifice.

the birth of secrets ocean deep with complicated reasons for
the keeping; the main one being it's just not that easy to talk
about some people... desires... fantasies... sectors of yourself...
with your "ONE AND ONLY" love.

d'much rather play love games.

that's better

than getting none of what

we want.

d'much rather play love games.

too much blood pumping through us low

too many thoughts, of which, we cannot just let go

too many beautiful people in the world

and of all the people in the world...

there is the attraction

that we feel even when

we control the subtraction.

so smile

and speak to me just above a whisper like you do

and miss me when you don't see me

and moan each time we touch

and dance around

the possibility

with me.

or walk away.

but the games never end

and I am too young

to know any better

and too new to the game

to know when to give up on a good thing.

now, stop playing. and stop asking me why I'm playing.

Love JM

Just because I love the way I do

Always have had a harder time

Not knowing if I would ever feel okay inside.

Everyday feeling like an outsider.

Like "they're watchin'"

Like "they're talkin' about me"

Every time they stared, I would overthink ME.

More than you know, you've changed my world.

One statement, song, fashion decision, interview, press release at a time.

No one can do you like you, girl.

And now I'm sure no one can do me like me.

Everything about "Dirty Computer" cultivates love.

20/20

Love is not blind.

In fact, it's got 20/20.

Now I know it can "take ova yo mind"

'Cause that's what you be doin' to me.

Love is not blind.

It's what allows me to see you for you.

Glasses tight, Gucci, just right

to protect my focus and view.

Love is not blind.

It's not a cyclops,

and it don't got cataracts eitha.

It can transcend space and time.

It's a promise maker and a promise keeper.

Love is not blind.

Optometrists agree.

It is to see the highest heights,

when love is what you see.

Love is not blind.

It exists, all senses engaged.

I wear glasses but I see you

walking right through love's parade.

"Played"

Getting played

for a fool

is one of the

worst feelings,

because it makes you

question how smart you really are?

or is it,

how dumb love can really make you?

Built Tough (a daughter-father poem)

She wishes

he held her

tight

and held onto her.

like that thin steering wheel.

and showed care.

like the clean streaks

across the wide windshield.

calmed her bruises.

like the rumbling, soft hum

of the young engine.

she wishes

she knew him.

like that grey coat of paint. one red stripe, one blue.

and he knew her.

like the get-up or the miles until empty.

and that they both saw themselves

in the rearview...

and from the side view mirrors too.

she wishes

he would come running

or pull up

finally.

and hold on

and show care

and calm her bruises.

she acts tough

because they

tell her that she looks it.

that she looks

tough enough.

to keep on.

loving him.

them.

regardless of if

he ever details

their love,

like that F-150 he used to,

before rust eats away at it all.

At them.

Where I'm from

All this time

I have just

been saying

that I am from Detroit.

Which I guess is true.

Mostly.

but then it can't be.

might be

one of those things

everybody knows and

just can't find the words to tell me.

like when they

thought

they had my queerness figured out

before me.

I am always

becoming

and realizing

and accepting

myself.

it is so cool

when someone

knows you well.

and it is so not cool

when a stranger thinks

they know you at all.

The Empress empties her heart here

With their truth

and their secrets,

it seems

they have love

that won't reach...

far enough around her

to be well-to-do.

Heartache

that won't ease

up

too.

And yet, the love that

beats on

inside them

drives her crazy.

She turns to run away...

. this is for her best interest.

you are where

preservation means severance.

away with

all remnants

images

communication.

"It's better that way,"

to fill

everything

with nothing.

"no" for "yes".

ignore the rest.

easier than

being in love.

"who has ever been better

off

without love?"

but with them

and their shape,

it seems

they are just.   too.   oblong.

.to fit into

.her best interest.

truth on mute.

secrets erased upstairs.

lips to yourself.

feels on the shelf.

love is

an omnipotent category of storm.

with no way

to prepare

for its touchdown,

self-preservation means

running in the opposite direction.

fast enough.

and, if.

for.

her.best.interest,

Never looking back.

If Zellia was your first love…

I hope she loved you right.

you feel like she learned you well.

and knew how to make you smile.

and laugh.

laughing is important.

…

I hope she was

present

for what

you had to offer.

and made you feel.

and showed you, you.

…

I hope you know

that

she still has all the sentimental things your heart gave her.

even if she never kept all the material things your money
bought her.

…

I hope

she told you stinging truths.

apologized if and

when she had not.

and told you stories.

the good kind, from her life.

....

I hope she admitted

when she

had been shacked up

in a lie

with you.

or when she made a bad day

for you two

your fault.

...

I hope her scent

finds you

unexpectedly

when you're alone or

most inappropriately

when you're in public.

...

you show up

in her poetry.

and in her

dreams at night time.

...

I hope you seek

for her essence

in other women.

and that you keep that part

a secret

so, your new will know you

never compare her

to the old.

...you have accepted

that

she is the bar.

You or Whatever

"The way you handle me..."

The way I handle you

has almost nothing

to do with

my hands...

Reasons by EW+F

The before-I-met-you moment

long gone   and

here,   after,

you are more beautiful

than you

seemed to be *then*.

Your aura and all.

                             the

way you receive me.

                             Love,

Getting you

off of my mind

is a   game

I have no tokens for.

No

one

thought   has

recurred like

the one of you.

My imagination has   been

reborn.

                             Played

around

up there

today,

with you... It was the remedy.

74

Gathering

Fell in love

with you

and all you could do

was run around

                                           gathering excuses

for why you

could not

love me back.

Feelings

and I'm not thirsty

for you anymore.

I don't seek

my thoughts for you.

I know you're not hiding

in the corners of my mind,

where I'd keep you

in between falls.

We've fallen all the way

apart.

used to gulp down water

just to clear the nervousness

at the back

of my throat

long enough to let out a decent greeting.

Now my feelings are mountains.

Tears are valleys

and I'm no hiker

so, I suppose

I'll never climb high enough

away from my mind

to get over you.

I only have

the memories left

to help me deal.

A Bad Difference

I just want to be able to lay with you always or whenever we want or need. But you don't need me. You only want me and only sometimes. Like less than part-time. I want you always. So, then there's the difference between you and me.

Centre

last night

I think I

fell in love with you.

It was after

we talked

about our childhoods.

how mine

was close to a fairytale

and yours

sometimes was

as cold as the north pole,

how alone

you felt.

in falling deeper,

in love with you

I feel the icebergs melting.

I feel you

drawing nearer to me.

last night

I could feel heat rising

from our sun rays.

it was like

I met you in...

at the...

middle of myself.

Felt like a kid again.

I was happy...

and you were warm

and with me.

First Class Mail

I think about you sometimes.

I can't just let it go,

I'm that type.

I can't just go on,

dismissing my every thought of you.

the s*** is hard.

why do I want to?

reach out to you

just to say that one sentence?

"I miss you."

I guess I just need to get busy enough

not to notice

my feelings any more.

I need to

get my life.

Dehydrated Fruit

...

all dried up but, by some means,

delectable upon swallowing.

I wish I could

taste the air

from that summer

when we really

loved each other

and would say it.

flip my sidekick open

to see your

digital sweet nothings.

and fall asleep,

dreaming that you

moved in with me

to stay.

cheeto stains on my cargos.

fruit punch lips kissing yours.

I want love

that's not afraid

to race home just before curfew,

if it means the most time with me.

windows down and eyes wide open.

tomorrow on their mind

as they park in the driveway,

right on time.

every time.

like your favorite snack.

Hunger Games

I don't want to

call it war,

what's going on inside me.

But there's

gun smoke

that won't clear

and I'm here...

no weapons...

no gear.

I want relief.

...

And then your "**look**"

saves me from

the savagery and edge

of it

all.

And the darkness

in my soul

gets clouded out

as our eyes lock.

You are my armor.

Like a blanket over quicksand.

this black handling by black hands

says to me

the worst has been survived.

And then I breathe 'cause

You're that custom fit savior

reclaiming me

redeeming me

from the lightlessness.

your last breaths,

clearing the gun smoke

from the district

that is my sensitivity.

No war,

but the sight of you

belts victory...

I swear.

If kisses could fly

I'd be their star pilot,

no cost for overhead, carry-on affection

Only the best seat selection...

for these kisses.

If kisses could fly

there'd be no reason why

hugs couldn't either and I'd hold you close

and long, if hugs could fly.

If kisses could fly,

we both know I

would feel much closer to you.

If kisses could fly,

I'd blow a bunch your way

to start your day.

If kisses could fly,

you'd have a gentle hummingbird's worth

waiting for you

when you sit down for coffee.

If kisses could fly

both you and I

would close the distance

between us.

Who Knows What May Happen

You slipped through my fingers

like punch lines or bars

or key points do

when you don't

write them down fast enough.

There were bigger ways

to have acknowledged you.

And just like fleeting thoughts,

you've never come

back around to me...

and there's no telling if you ever will

swing back

into my life's path

somehow.

I tell myself

I would not

let you

slip through again.

would hold on tighter to you.

would write you down.

Never got to you though...

and probably never will get to...

Little

I wish I

thought of you

that much.

A small amount.

And I don't know

if it's anger

or just plain disappointment

when I think

of you.

Maybe it's that

I'm mad

at myself

for not being able

to forgive you

and mad at myself

for lying

about loving you

for who you really

were.

I loved you

for the idea

of who I wanted

and needed

you to be...

and I loved

how you affected me.

In many ways

you empowered me

to look in on myself,

to dare to change myself too,

in whatever ways

I want. Wanted.

I thought that

by trying to control you,

I could also control

our fate.

The future of us

was never mine to decide.

Not even a little.

A Bootleg Forcefield

I woke up

to a partition

between us.

One that I did not

place, nor did I,

though somewhat shocked and maybe moreso displeased to find it there,

feel inclined to remove.

For even if it

weren't there,

I'm not sure I'd trust you

with my body heat

anyhow.

Not sure what you holding me would even mean.

 And even *with*

a severance of the mattress,

you were a pillow

or three

away from me

and yet I felt so alone

in that bed.

Why did you separate us like so?

And do I truly care,

the reason?

The distance

between us

was in need of illustration,

it seems. Did I

get in your way

with *all of myself*

there in bed

with you?

I wish my body

would have slept

until morning

and then I would have only had to see it once.

The partition

that you put there

between us.

A note on love hurting #38

If heartbreak

could be swallowed

I'd digested you

by now

and left you

to continue draining

to a sewer line

I'll never see or know.

Gone forever

Like when I flushed this morning.

Heartbreak memo #3,479

I am so very grateful for my memory. If not for it, you'd be nothing more than the cry. Nothing more than how heartbreak tingles on my tongue.

Mastering the body comes naturally when the love for *it* is real... the hands are of someone who loves *you* and touches *you* like so...

What's problematic is how bad I wish *your* heart... would have told *mine* that it never stood a chance. Too focused on other organs. Now look at us. And not with your eyes, with your heart and mind, like I'm doing right now.

Emotionally Flagrant (Love and Basketball)

In love's court,

I am exactly

where I should live.

And so,

when you casted me away,

if felt like a bloody foul.

and what made it worse

was you

throwing your hands up in the air

like

you were innocent.

like

there was no harm done.

In love's court,

there are no referees.

there's only me to come to my defense.

A Single Rose

and my heart flutters

at the sight

of your garden's space.

I believe

all is in order,

though I never knew your preferences.

the weeds

are few.

and in time,

the leaves too.

always ready

for you to show up

and show out.

like how you made

those tulips

burst in the front yard.

and a single rose

spring up again,

in the back.

you are everywhere.

Pre-Sorted

if fate brought us together

then

fate's what ripped us

apart.

and if I was genuinely destined

to,

I'd have the key to your heart.

But there is no master

key.

You're hard to break open and

unlock.

Smile as soft as sunrise, soul as hard as

rock.

if I was meant to be with

you

I think, in love, you and I would

be.

I would not have to beg and plead for you to be with

me.

if fate brought us together

then

fate's what ripped us

apart.

you think we had zero control

over

our own decisions, from the

start?

Happy Enough

they look like

they might last

a while.

they look good

together.

And I'm not one to fall

for the look

of a thing

right fast.

socialization tells me

not to be excited for her.

the lover in me

can't help herself.

even though

I used to be the one

on her arm,

the new look

fits her well too.

maybe better

but I'll never know

unless she tells me.

I can only look on.

from my vantage point,

the coast looks clear

and they look happy enough

to sail on in love.

H.E.R.

Your voice

escorts the sun

each morning it rises.

It can make

thoughts grow

like weeds do

between the sidewalk blocks.

In the hood,

where there's blight

and moreover abandon,

your pour of

sultry

is like

a salve

to loveless wounds.

In a mind

where memories have insomnia

and there's sometimes mourning...

over breakfast

your notes carry

and stick

like dried syrup on ceramic.

Your singing is needed.

You... singing...

can make

tears fall

that dry themselves up.

At the sound of you,

love is remembered.

At the sound of you,

love is now.

You make everything

okay again

when you sing.

You make me

so grateful

that my record had a SIDE-B.

Know When to Surrender

Woke up to you...

with that look on your face.

The same one

you had

when we fell into

a kissing fit

last night,

in the middle of the night.

Eyes full of sentence fragments

and morse code

and all the sounds of approval

you fought to

keep in,

with a balled-up fist...

over those full lips.

Skin telling me

that your

temperature's rising...

chocolate

melted in the sheets

and left to harden.

The morning

is filled with endless avenues

and travel based on the

flexibility

you submit

for review.

Peeling back

the comforter

for more cocoa...

with that look, in my eyes.

Like

I need it now.

No need

to point me

in the right direction.

I know.

And "good morning".

Xerox

Never is a long time.

Had me doin' things

I'd *never* done

and have *never* done since.

And sometimes I want that back.

The way you had me doing things.

Seeing and being

things

all new.

And it's only you

that can do that...

all that...

to me.

Never is a long time.

You once said

I did

the same to you.

Made you feel brand new.

And...

To think that

you and I

will never be.

And if you're

over there crying

like I do, lightly, at the remembrance of us...

it's only because

you're a copycat.

To heal you

"Gracious words are like a honeycomb, sweetness to the soul and health to the body." Proverbs 16:24

you were sleeping

when I held my hand

to your forehead

and gave you

all my hope.

your breaths

were labored.

light lines of sweat

moistening your

cheeks and upper lip.

I gave you

all my energy,

cupping your skull

under my palm.

the room was quiet,

except for my heart

telling me not to let go

yet.

I gave you

my strength,

needing to see you

get to the other side

of your conditions.

I said a prayer...

you'd find rest...

and you'd find

layers

of healing

and restoration

and you'd feel my love

even in your sleep.

A Thousand Years

We must have

loved

and let go

of one another,

a thousand years ago.

"Don't Take *It* Personal"

which part?

what happened

or what's happening now?

because it all feels

quite personal

to me.

what other ways

are there

to take or receive

all of this?

Rhetorically Speaking

What's the point of cards and letters

if they'll only

get thrown away...

disowned

like the love was never there...

if we're over?

If there were a certain amount

of tears you could cry, to fix a certain thing,

how many times would I have cried as much as it took?

What's left of a photograph that depicts a "forever" that has met its end? because "forever" never does that—can't end. Can't.

How would I look longing for something long gone, instead of just taking today for all that it is?

Don't answer that. I'm fine.

Although Fall is my favorite season

Spring was supposed to be here.

And everyone feels how the weather cannot decide.

Or maybe it's deeper than deciding?

These Days are cold and rainy.

These Days are dragging their feet through snow… drifting

further away from change.

Nights

are days

that were too tired to get out of bed.

These Days are absent-minded and

Seniors are sitting up straight,

wanting to see the bulbs blossom

and become the spring-forwardness

the D is missing.

Maybe the season's onset is just running late.

and then Spring is here for me…

even inside a building,

as I see you smile.

Made up s***

There's really no such thing as

"the middle of the night".

There's just asleep and awake.

And I am awake.

I am thinking about you.

And I think about you all the time.

And there's really no such thing as "time".

But I hope you believe all this anyway.

Half this s*** in "life" is made up.

The way I feel though,

at the thought of you,

well that

just "now"

came to be.

What's more real than   n   o   w

I can't think of anything...

Taste as you go

You stay mad

that I want to

check in with you,

here and again,

about the way I feel.

Mad that

I always

have some feelings that need to be said.

I just want us

to

turn out right.

Although this will not read like heartbreak

when we're alone

even the sirens are inaudible noise—

all I hear is you.

I am stuck

in the way

of the way you look at me…

just looking…

and pleased to do just and only that.

Who am I in your eyes that

the basic

feels expert-level-real

when I'm with you?

A peck of a kiss and there's glitter.

Your hands on my thighs and there's sparkling rain.

I am stuck,

standing still and

holding a vase full of

flowers made out of all the love games you play.

the adjective You are

this love story feels like hittin' snooze while hearing rain move the trees. just outside the bedroom window. in this love, all toes tucked under and moaning to be kept merely more minutes in your arms. You set me so free. some days it feels like espresso in my veins, seeing you. your eyes are the color of agape and your whispers smell like the desire I hold space for. I've never felt someone look through me. scared of how good us is but counting it all joy, with flushed pupils and hot cheeks. and if only I could can our yesterdays in glass and… make strawberry jam out of the way I can never rinse away your high completely. I want to untighten our sealed mason jars in every season. You in all your Shine. Such an unobstructed stream we've been kneeling beside. Water… the way I need you in me. Such a blameless intrigue we've been raising. Honey… the way I drizzle you all over the parts of My Life turned merciless. When you part your lips to speak to me, you set me so free. And I've never felt someone look through me. And if only I could can—You in all your Shine. Irresistible a$$…

Trippin'

you find function

in dysfunction.

I only find the dys-

you crawl under

our standing

so when I get it,

you always mis-

understand me when I say that this is it for you and me.

Loop Mail

I love chocolate skin.

the way it

looks like candy,

moisturized.

the way it

starts summer over

in my mind.

and everything

that you put on

is just a bowl

for the fudge.

enough sun and I can

loop my spoon in

for seconds.

COA

we make

time collapse.

then we lose

our place in it.

gone for miles.

deep in our own nile.

this is it,

our lovemaking scene

and

every

need

for

a

change of address.

A Stack of 3

pancakes...

just as soon as I

finally

learned to make them perfectly,

I had

no one

but myself

to make them for.

we were over.

and making breakfast

brought you to mind.

along with

all the other dope things

you taught me how to do.

Fell for you

My legs still feel weak baby

      Your legs still feel weak baby?

Yea... Crazy.

      What happened?

I think I fell... yea... I think I fell.

ten years in ten seconds

it's been a decade

since we last

made love.

and when we embrace

it does not feel like

yesterday again.

but to everyone

who sees us,

we look

in love all over again.

and that has to be

because

it's always been real,

the way I feel

when I see you.

Whatever is Whatever

Tibetan Freedom Concert Planning

a mix cd worth keeping,

is made with more than

time spent thinking.

songs chosen are...

loved.

a fella could

make a girl double-back

and decide to dance,

choosing right on the juke box.

the right record

spinning under the needle,

is like an intravenous solution...

the way you feel it in you.

music is

words and melody

and

sound

competing

for your heart.

a mix cd worth keeping

has hidden meanings

on its custom tracks.

interludes like scrapbooks.

songs chosen

are the brilliant things

we can never seem to think of

ourselves...

or the ways

we fail to be

present, forgiving, clever, mindful, vulnerable.

music is a gift of love,

for love,

from love.

Dear "Straight Girl"

Don't worry, I'll keep this brief. If you were so "straight", you wouldn't keep staring at me like that. All up and down and more than once. And me being "unstraight" doesn't mean I think you're cute. But you are. Stop staring at me and go *get a woman to make **a** love with.*

All Love,

Zee

Dear "Straight Girl" PT. 2

The taste of her

cherry chapstick

is long gone

by the time the orgasms arrive.

what was a kiss

turned into

lovemaking

and from love

there is no hiding.

Now we got "straight girl" problems.

Plebeian Thoughts

It's a new millennium

and money

cannot buy

immortality

and everyone's confused

about what's taking

technology so long

to learn how to

make us live forever.

In this plutocracy,

play dress up and

don't play

when it comes to the money,

honey.

or else...

They say "Time is Money"

He said

he was

stuck in traffic

but that

it didn't matter

because he was

making a lot more money

nowadays.

I guess

once you have

enough of it,

you just don't have to

care as much,

about certain things.

Time lost,

in his case.

He can now afford to waste time,

because he makes enough money to…

Ha!

The Magic Hour

"Man, alone chimes the hour. And, because of this, man suffers a paralyzing fear that no other creature endures. A fear of time running out." - Mitch Albom

From the moment

we first open our eyes,

we are propitious.

Our lives will continuously

cocoon

and eclose.

Sometimes

with expectation.

Most times,

with wonderment.

It is by means of wisdom

that we learn...

what miracles *look* like,

what grace and mercy *feel* like,

what the world

tastes like with *love* in it.

Ambrosial --

e v e r y t h i n g, a bit sweeter...

Seraphic even...

Like how the blue

of the night

cruises into the yellow

of the morning

when the sun is due

to rise.

... how the orange

of the day

marries the purple

of the night,

at sunset.

The minute

we close our eyes

for the last time,

we are fortunate.

To have seen the stars

shift shape

and the universe

abide

and breathe back.

To have dreamt dreams

then lived them.

To have grown

Love...

absent of conditions,

escaping time eternally.

To have cradled

unique imaginings in our minds,

blessings in our arms.

Our lives will continuously

cocoon

and eclose.

Sunrise and sunset

look like twins in the sky,

at the magic hour.

No one can name

which

is more beautiful.

Missent

when you were here,

I always wanted to ask you

certain questions...

to make you answer them.

when you were here,

I always wanted explanations

or apologies

or some t h i n g.

I wanted you to talk

about what I wanted

to talk about

and I wanted you to listen too.

Never asked

so you never answered.

Never dared

to challenge you

to say some real s***.

or to listen to me

spit the real

to you.

and now that

you're gone,

I have all this courage

and fearlessness

to speak.

I thought my thoughts

about it all

would have left

when you did.

Dear Syd

I found out that

She

loves

you

for

a whole 'notha set of reasons.

Your Song

In line at the bank.

Lines of you in the banks of my body.

The Bank will break

if I wish too hard

to have you back, here, next to me in line.

Your song is on

and I mouth

the words.

What an unexpected withdrawal.

Real

Love isn't always pretty.

Like the weather...

Like sailing on the sea...

When it gets rough

It *seems*

That's what makes it real.

Like a baby

through the isms

and the manifestos.

when all there's

ever left to do

is try to

figure out

how

or

why.

where the lights

are dead

and kids have stopped

becoming.

through the flames

and the screams.

when not even church

or school is safe.

the bullets

and the beatings

and the bars

and the boys becoming

men

behind

them.

Please tell me

I am not alone

when I cry for the world.

I want to

buy justice with this

wet face,

like they do in the movies.

I want to

ask America—

"America, how do you sleep?"

… and America would answer,

"Well, obviously…"

Running Water (fake American woes)

If the water's

not hot enough,

I'll stand there

and wait

a while.

Because I've got time.

I'll run my hand

back and forth

through the stream

until the

temperature

is just how I love it.

Because it's my shower.

And then I'll step in...

and stay for as many

lather-and-rinse

rounds

as I want.

or I might just run a bath instead.

Because I can.

I'll check to make sure

the temperature is right

then too.

Nothing's worse

than a bathtub

full of water

that's too hot.

X MARKS THE SPOT

Some people go back

to their exes

for the same reason

most people don't—

there is no one like them

in all the earth.

Whether that's

good or bad

is always the question...

always the root of deciding.

Instagram

But you

double-tapped

in your mind though.

Thrifting is like love at first sight

love is like

a thrift store find.

the way It makes you feel giddy.

so happy that you found It

you are smitten

and you pause

to thank the universe

for a blessing it somehow

knew you needed.

you didn't know

or you had forgotten

about the need.

It doesn't have to be

from

where you're from—

you don't care.

you take It home

you give It TLC and

It becomes yours

to do with what you will,

for sure.

It feels like

It hasn't cost you

a thing.

House of Cards

What an unbelievable last name…

There has never been one more defining

for the leader of the free world.

what a gigantic flood of failure

in such a small amount of time.

Let's see someone

trump

that.

"It's Your World"

white man.

older.

with his entitlement.

does not bother

to look both ways before crossing

the street.

the walkway

looked both ways for him,

I guess.

white couple.

older than the pedestrian.

with their entitlement.

does not bother

to slow down or

to look both ways

as they approach

the crosswalk.

white man

keeps walking.

white couple

keeps rolling.

and once they cancel

each other out,

with their selfishness

and disregard,

I will proceed

to drive ahead

to the store.

the couple makes a hard stop.

I laugh.

"It's your world!"

Mourning Sickness

Your mornings were not made for this.

Trust that the way you feel is only temporary.

Apologies don't take away the pain.

The Casio

I had a box of watches

I threw away.

I was trying to forget

everything

about the concept of time.

I just want my body

to respond to

the sunrise and sunsets,

the scents and sights,

the shifts and stops.

I am exhausted

just merely thinking

that I may have

run out of it.

Who am I,

thinking I can

trap the hands of the day

inside this

fancy jewelry piece

and view it on my wrist?

manage its strike.

ha.

one day, they'll be people

again

that just don't

believe in time.

you just watch!

Be Yourself

It can't be that hard, right?

Tell me it is, if so.

For you to dress the way you want.

to go where you go.

It can't be that hard, right?

You just being you.

Rockin' that hairstyle.

Wearin' those shoes.

your life perspectives,

your imagination too.

no one on the planet

is just like you.

So Be Yourself

because it's a role

only you can fill.

Life is so much easier

when you

keep it real.

Bundles

self- awareness, self-love, emotional intelligence, understanding, imagination, self- expression, resourcefulness, education, intellect, creativity, passion, kindness, determination, pride, joy, perseverance, generosity, patience, wisdom, faith, honesty, eagerness, work ethic, sensitivity, empathy, respect... the whole package, in excess.

Christmas on Braile St.

she coiled her love around

the banister

and she could

make the walls sing.

everyone was alright.

boxes and bows in sight.

she let her love let her labor

overnight

and she cooked everything just right.

That scene...

music playing

and the weight of their marriage

slow dancing

in the living room

with them.

the gifts

I loved the most

had no wrapping paper at all.

They are the moments

I hold close

to my heart,

older and with my own tree to decorate.

"What's wrong with being pretty?"

Well,

most times,

it's not knowing

just how pretty

you really are.

Detroit (My Lover)

So big

but you be

feelin' so small sometimes.

Feels like

we grow wide

more than

we grow tall sometimes.

we have been through

our fair share.

car missing,

kicks stolen and

I still care.

I can see the glean

from your glow-up

sometimes.

So old

but you be feelin'

so young sometimes.

Feels like

we get let down

more than we have fun sometimes.

holiday shell casings

during fireworks

for years consecutive.

nothin' will ruin me or make me speculative.

I can see

the grand in your

finale, in the

graffiti in the alley sometimes.

you're so prestigious

but you be feelin' so hood.

coney so bad

but you be tastin' so good.

so mild

but they say you be feelin' so cold.

show love

but you be feelin' so bold.

so sweet

but you be feelin' so mean.

so dirty

in parts where you used to be clean.

so "set back"

yet the face and force of innovation.

so sorry

that capitalism brings your declination.

they call it gentrification.

time to change the station

to some Detroit radio.

Talent Acquisition

Life is real different

when you know

your strength and weaknesses.

'Cause then

no one can tell you

what yo weakness is.

The world,

don't gotta tell you

how bleak it is.

Way worse once they find out

what yo secrets is.

See life is

just a word

to describe the things

that the puppets can do

strings or no strings.

that the nature mother does

to make the birds sing.

the hard times

certain predicaments bring.

But see life is helly different

when you livin'

what yo purpose is.

then you can wear yo heart

on yo shirt and s***.

speak up or cry out

when you hurt and s***.

ride front seat,

smoke da purp and s***.

And the pain

is just a side effect.

careful, your condition.

can't be comforted by complaint

or by petition.

blessings pourin' down

just gotta stay in position.

See, life is just Talent Acquisition.

An excerpt from the soon to be released novel entitled *"Just in case the world ends"* by Zellia E. Fossett

The first time Addison and Remi made love, not even the heavens saw it coming. The lovemaking blew by, like a summer breeze through the windows of a ranch style home, and they'd been ass naked in the middle of the kitchen floor. Addison never knew where they were, until it was over and both women were reaching out for one another and for air too, and fingertips were meeting cabinet ends and bends. The entire ordeal had started so innocently and continued so sensually that it never once felt like sex. It felt like something *beyond* it. It didn't feel like "adultery" either, Addison was no infidel, let her tell it. It felt like what was *supposed to be* happening. Before they made love, Addison's attraction to women was a well-kept and fulfilling secret. After they came up, Remi felt more like a decision she would have to make. Addison instantly wanted both Remi and Jude for keeps and she could not explain to herself how trying to keep them both seemed like it'd be more fulfilling than just choosing one love over the other for her forever.

Addison was still married to her husband because she loved him. Everything about their relationship too, except for the distance from time to time. He was intellectual, handsome, loving and promised her he'd always stay fit just to be sure he could protect her and live long with her. He was silly and he was always on time; for work, for appointments, for dates and outings, just always. She loved the way he behaved when something was really important to him; with patient attention and a sort of smooth, even-paced aggression. His obsessive nature helped him to learn her ins and outs in no time, he had nearly mastered her when they first fell in love. Now, they were a small, loving family and she was happy. In recent years,

Jude was hardly ever home and his absence gave her space and time to learn herself better.

Jude was still married to Addison because he loved her. Everything about her. He dealt with the growing fear of dying alone like his own father and favorite uncle had done in their early sixties. He could not leave her or rather chose not to fathom life without her, because she was so good to him, for him. She was so very beautiful to him and had been a partner and mother in capacities that never fell short of impressive. He also, after spending lengths of time away for work, was becoming more uncomfortable with the idea of there being so much distance sometimes. It made him want to hold on and never let go, when they hugged while making breakfast together. It made him thrust deep and slow, when they made love for hours it seemed. The distance made him miss his wife and his children… miss his life. And every time he came back home he'd be driven to tears just by the scent of her hair. It was as if he had no life without her. There was nothing, always, until he came home.

Later that month

He exited the truck and almost ran to the side door of the house. Midnight wasn't too far off and he knew the kids were in bed. He put his bags down near the door, kicked off his oxfords and walked into the kitchen. She was there, waiting for him.

"I've missed you so much and you look so good, Addi. I missed you baby," Jude rushed her way but quietly.

"You look pretty nice yourself, young sir. You know I've missed you so!" She grabbed and pulled him nearer by his waist.

Jude held Addison close and kissed her in the center of her scalp. He rocked back and forth gently and held on. She folded into his muscular chest and felt tears swell in her eyes, at the encompassing scent of his cologne. Jude had been gone for four months, half way across the country. He'd be back in town for two months then gone again for another four. She held onto him tighter. They kissed the way they do.

"Where are they? In their rooms?" Jude pretended to listen out for child-like sounds.

"You know it. Or in the basement guest room. We expected you earlier. Once I saw your flight was delayed, they all went their own ways. You can say 'hi' at breakfast if you're worried you'll wake them but they stay up on their phones all night sometimes," Addison rolled her eyes playfully.

"I'll wait until the morning. I can think of other things I need to handle around this house. Let me get cleaned up." Jude smiled and stared into her eyes.

"Oh no, don't worry. Let me handle it all for you," she pushed him against the refrigerator and traced her hand down to his crotch. As he let out a low gasp, she grabbed his right hand and lead him into their master bathroom for a long bath and a massage after.

Raising their three children was not easy. Addison was often pulled in multiple directions at once but she managed well, even her emotions and moods. The boys, as they grew older, became sketchier and more secretive while it seemed her quiet daughter began to open and bloom and share herself with age. Addison was for sure more worried about her sons than her daughter, because she'd caught them red-handed, in so many arenas of life, and it was hard to seriously trust them. The plan was for the family to enjoy one another every time they were together. The plan was for Jude to retire once their youngest child, Chase, met his first year of college. They felt quite confident he would do well on his own because even though he was the youngest of the three, he proved to absolutely be the smartest.

To be continued...

I Love
you
See ya
Love always
Di

CPSIA information can be obtained
at www.ICGtesting.com
Printed in the USA
FFHW021128281018
48988892-53244FF